Classic Prayers

For:

Rejoice always,

pray without ceasing, in everything give thanks;
for this is the will of God in Christ Jesus for you.

1 Thessalonians 5:16–18
New King James Version

From:

Late summer on the farm, Fife

*Every Christian needs a half-hour of prayer each day,
except when he is busy, then he needs an hour.*

Francis de Sales (1567–1622), Bishop of Geneva

Prayers
FOR EVERYDAY LIFE

OLD SARUM
Prayer

God be in my head and in my understanding;

God be in my eyes and in my looking;

God be in my mouth and in my speaking;

God be in my heart and in my thinking;

God be at my end and at my departing.

This prayer first appeared in the **Sarum Primer in 1514,**
Sarum being the name of an early settlement close to modern-day Salisbury.

Climbing Ben A'an, Trossachs

Miniature rose bud

SAINT PATRICK'S Prayer

*A*s I arise today,

may the strength of God pilot me,

the power of God uphold me,

the wisdom of God guide me.

May the eye of God look before me,

the ear of God hear me,

the word of God speak for me.

May the hand of God protect me,

the way of God lie before me,

the shield of God defend me,

the host of God save me.

May Christ shield me today.

Christ with me, Christ before me,

Christ behind me,

Christ in me, Christ beneath me,

Christ above me,

Christ on my right, Christ on my left,

Christ when I lie down, Christ when I sit,

Christ when I stand,

Christ in the heart of everyone who thinks of me,

Christ in the mouth of everyone who speaks of me,

Christ in every eye that sees me,

Christ in every ear that hears me.

Amen

Saint Patrick (387–493) was born in Roman Britain. At the age of sixteen Patrick was captured by Irish raiders and deported to Ireland where he was enslaved as a herdsman. During his six years as a slave his faith deepened, he eventually escaped and returned to his family. Later, he was ordained a Bishop and returned to Ireland.

Prayers from the
GELASIAN SACRAMENTARY

*I*nto your hands, merciful Lord,

we commend ourselves for this day;

may we be aware of your presence until its end;

remind us that in whatever good we do we are serving you;

make us careful and watchful,

so that in everything we may discern your will,

and, knowing it, may gladly obey.

The Gelasian Sacramentary is an 8th-century book of Christian liturgy
that contains priests' texts for celebrating Eucharist throughout the year.
An old tradition linked the book to Pope Gelasius I, the 5th-century pope.

OUR MORNING STAR

O God, our morning star

Splendour of light eternal

Shining with the glory of the rainbow

Come and waken us from the greyness of our apathy

And renew in us your gift of hope.

Amen

Saint Bede the Venerable (672–735)
An English monk at the Northumbrian monastery of Saint Peter.
He is well known as an author and scholar, and his most famous
work, *The Ecclesiastical History of the English People* gained
him the title 'The Father of English History'.

Sunrise over Queen's Park, Glasgow

Visiting the fields, Chittagong Hill Tracts, Bangladesh

THE GRAIL
Prayer

*L*ord Jesus,

I give you my hands to do your work.

I give you my feet to go your way.

I give you my eyes to see as you do.

I give you my tongue to speak your words.

I give you my mind that you may think in me.

I give you my spirit that you may pray in me.

Above all,

I give you my heart that you may love in me

your Father and all mankind.

I give you my whole self that you may grow in me,

so that it is you, Lord Jesus,

who live and work and pray in me.

Used with permission of The Grail

THE LORD'S PRAYER

Our Father in heaven,

Hallowed be Your name.

Your kingdom come.

Your will be done

On earth as it is in heaven.

Give us this day our daily bread.

And forgive us our debts,

As we forgive our debtors.

And do not lead us into temptation,

But deliver us from the evil one.

For Yours is the kingdom

and the power and the glory forever.

Amen

Matthew 6:9–13 New King James Version.
This is the prayer that Jesus taught his disciples.

Looking up Catacol Glen, Isle of Arran

On *earth* as it is in *heaven* • Our *Father* in heaven • *Hallowed* be Your name

Harvest Time, Fife

CELTIC BLESSING

May there always be work for your hands to do.
May your purse always hold a coin or two.
May the sun always shine upon your window pane.
May a rainbow be certain to follow each rain.
May the hand of a friend always be near to you and
May God fill your heart with gladness to cheer you.

Traditional Celtic Blessing

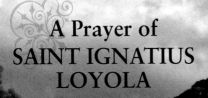

A Prayer of
SAINT IGNATIUS
LOYOLA

Teach us, good Lord,

to serve you as you deserve;

to give and not to count the cost;

to fight and not to heed the wounds;

to toil and not to seek for rest;

to labour and not to ask for any reward,

save that of knowing that we do your will.

Saint Ignatius Loyola (1491–1556) was a Spanish knight from a noble family. After being seriously wounded in battle he became a Christian, gave up his military life and devoted himself to working for God.

View from the train, near Lenzie

A Prayer of
SAINT TERESA
OF ÁVILA

Christ has no body now, but yours.

No hands, no feet on earth, but yours.

Yours are the eyes through which he looks

With compassion on this world.

Let nothing disturb you.

Let nothing frighten you.

All things pass away:

God never changes.

Patience obtains all things.

Those who have God

Find they lack nothing;

God alone suffices.

Saint Teresa of Ávila (1515–1582)
At the age of 16, Teresa was a rebel and her
disciplinarian father sent her to a convent where she
found she had more freedom than she did at home.
Eventually, after a severe illness that left her paralysed
for three years, she immersed herself in God – she
then had a vision of 'the sorely wounded Christ' that
changed her life forever.

Pink blossom in Glasgow Botanical Gardens

Lochranza Castle, Isle of Arran

Prayer of a
CONFEDERATE
SOLDIER

I asked God for strength that I might achieve,

I was made weak that I might learn humbly to obey.

I asked for health that I might do great things.

I was given infirmity that I might do better things.

I asked for riches that I might be happy.

I was given poverty that I might be wise.

I asked for power that I might have the praise of men.

I was given weakness that I might feel the need of God.

I asked for all things that I might enjoy life.

I was given life that I might enjoy all things.

I got nothing that I asked for – but everything that I had hoped for.

Almost despite myself, my unspoken prayers were answered.

I am, among all men, most richly blessed.

This prayer was found in the uniform pocket of a wounded,
battle-weary, Confederate States Army soldier near the end of the
United States Civil War c.1865.

God in my
DAILY LIFE

God to enfold me,
God to surround me,
God in my speaking,
God in my thinking.

God in my sleeping,
God in my waking,
God in my watching,
God in my hoping.

God in my life,
God in my lips,
God in my soul,
God in my heart.

God in my sufficing,
God in my slumber,
God in my ever-living soul,
God in mine eternity.

From **The Carmina Gadelica** – an anthology of Scottish prayers, poems, blessings and more, from the Celtic Oral tradition collected by Alexander Carmichael (1832–1912)

Sledging heaven, Queen's Park, Glasgow

Snowy path, Queen's Park, Glasgow

Prayers
OF THANKSGIVING

A Prayer of
SAINT RICHARD
OF CHICHESTER

*T*hanks be to you, our Lord Jesus Christ,

for all the benefits which you have given me,

for all the pains and insults which you have borne for me.

Most merciful Redeemer, Friend and Brother,

may I know you more clearly,

love you more dearly,

and follow you more nearly.

Saint Richard of Chichester (1197–1253)
Richard came from a wealthy farming family, but both his parents died while he was young and the farm fell into ruin. He worked hard to restore his family's fortune. He studied at Oxford University where he later became Chancellor before eventually being elected Bishop of Chichester.

Flowers in the field, Isle of Arran

THE SELKIRK GRACE

Some hae meat and canna eat,
And some wad eat that want it;
But we hae meat and we can eat,
Sae let the Lord be thankit.

(Traditional)

*S*ome have meat and cannot eat,

And some want to eat but have nothing;

But we have meat and we can eat,

So let's thank the Lord.

(Translation)

A mealtime grace used at Burns Night gatherings
in Scotland. This prayer was made popular by
Robert Burns (Scottish poet 1759–1796)

THE JOHNNY APPLESEED
Grace

Oh, the Lord is good to me
and so I thank the Lord
for giving me the things I need
the sun and the rain and the apple seed.
The Lord is good to me.

And every seed that grows
will grow into a tree,
and one day soon there'll be apples there,
for everyone in the world to share.
The Lord is good to me.

When I wake up each morning,
I'm happy as can be,
because I know that with God's care
the apple trees will still be there.
The Lord's been good to me.

Traditional Scout mealtime grace. **Johnny Appleseed** was the nickname for **John Chapman** (1774–1845) who worked as an apprentice in his local orchard. At 18 he set out for Western Pennsylvania with a bag of apple seeds. He grew plenty of apple trees and sold the saplings to the settlers so that they could have fresh fruit. He also planted many orchards of his own.

THANKSGIVING
Prayer

*F*or each new morning with its light,
For rest and shelter of the night,
For health and food,
For love and friends,
For everything Thy goodness sends.

Ralph Waldo Emerson (1803–1882)
American essayist, lecturer and poet.

North Glen Sannox, Isle of Arran

Prayers
FOR PEACE

BLESSING
Prayer

May the LORD bless you
and protect you.
May the LORD smile on you
and be gracious to you.
May the LORD show you his favour
and give you his peace.

Numbers 6:24–26, New Living Translation

Birch wood near Samara, Russia

Waterfall behind Catacol Farm

The Prayer of
SAINT FRANCIS OF ASSISI

*L*ord, make me an instrument of your **peace**.
Where there is hatred, let me sow **love**,
Where there is injury, **pardon**,
Where there is doubt, **faith**,
Where there is despair, **hope**,
Where there is darkness, **light**,
Where there is sadness, **joy**.

O Divine Master, grant that I may not so much
seek to be consoled as to console,
not so much to be understood as to understand,
not so much to be loved, as to love;
for it is in giving that we receive,
it is in pardoning that we are pardoned,
it is in dying that we awake to eternal life.

Saint Francis of Assisi (1182–1226)
Italian Catholic friar and preacher. He was the son of
a wealthy cloth merchant and enjoyed a good time.
While going off to war in 1204, he had a vision that
directed him back to Assisi, where he lost his taste for
the high life. He started preaching on the street and soon
amassed a following.

Isle of Arran from Ardrossan

A Prayer for
INNER PEACE

Deep peace of the running waves to you,

Deep peace of the flowing air to you,

Deep peace of the quiet earth to you,

Deep peace of the shining stars to you,

Deep peace of the gentle night to you,

Moon and stars always giving light to you.

Deep peace of Christ, the light of the world, to you.

Ancient Celtic Prayer

Into the distance, Catacol, Isle of Arran

Prayers
FOR GUIDANCE

A Prayer of
SAINT COLUMBA

*B*e, Lord Jesus,

a **bright flame** before me,

a **guiding star** above me,

a **smooth path** below me,

a **kindly shepherd** behind me:

today, tonight, and forever.

Saint Columba (521–597) was an Irish missionary monk and one of the
Twelve Apostles of Ireland. Columba is the patron saint of Derry,
Ireland, where he founded a monastic settlement circa. 540.

THE HELMSMAN

Steer the ship of my life, good Lord, to your quiet harbour,

where I can be safe from the storms of sin and conflict.

Show me the course I should take.

Renew in me the gift of discernment,

so that I can always see the right direction in which I should go.

And give me the strength and the courage to choose the right course,

even when the sea is rough and the waves are high,

knowing that through enduring hardship and danger in your name

we shall find comfort and peace.

Saint Basil of Caesarea (330-379)
The Greek bishop of Caesarea Mazaca in Cappadocia (modern-day Turkey). Basil was an eloquent
theologian and well-known for his care of the poor and needy.

Show me the right path, O Lord;

point out the road for me to follow.

Lead me by your truth and teach me,

for you are the God who saves me.

All day long I put my hope in you.

Psalm 25:4–5, New Living Translation

Ardrossan lighthouse

Prayers
FOR WISDOM

A Prayer of
SAINT THOMAS AQUINAS

*B*estow upon me, O Lord my God,

an understanding that knows thee,

wisdom in finding thee,

a way of life that is pleasing to thee,

perseverance that faithfully waits for thee,

and confidence that I shall embrace thee at the last.

Saint Thomas Aquinas (1225–1274)
An Italian Dominican priest and one of 33 Doctors of the Church. His parents,
the Count of Aquino and Countess of Teano, were not too happy that their
son had chosen to become a poor friar and they had him confined in a fortress
for almost two years while they attempted to talk him out of his vocation.

Staircase in St Bridget's Kirk, Fife

Berries in the snow

I have been driven many times to my knees by the overwhelming conviction that I had nowhere else to go. My own wisdom, and that of all about me, seemed insufficient for the day.

Abraham Lincoln (1809–1865), 16th President of the United States of America

The Prayer of
SAINT BENEDICT

Gracious and holy Father,
please give me:

> intellect to understand you;
>
> reason to discern you;
>
> diligence to seek you;
>
> wisdom to find you;
>
> a spirit to know you;
>
> a heart to meditate upon you;
>
> ears to hear you;
>
> eyes to see you;
>
> a tongue to proclaim you;
>
> a way of life pleasing to you;
>
> patience to wait for you;
>
> and perseverance to look for you.

Grant me:

> a perfect end,
>
> your holy presence,
>
> a blessed resurrection,
>
> and life everlasting.

Saint Benedict of Nursia (c.480–543)
Founded 12 communities for monks at
Subiaco in Italy. He was a gentle, disciplined
abbot. Today he is often called the founder
of Western monasticism.

Hiding in the treetops

The
DOXOLOGY

Praise God, from whom all blessings flow;

Praise Him, all creatures here below;

Praise Him above, ye heavenly host;

Praise Father, Son, and Holy Ghost.

The word 'doxology' comes from two Greek words, *doxa*, which means: 'glory or praise' and *legein*, which means: 'to speak.' So, doxology means "to speak of His glory." The words above are the last verse of the hymn, 'Awake, My Soul', written by **Thomas Ken (1637–1711)**.

DAVID'S PSALM
OF PRAISE

O Lord, our Lord,
your majestic name fills the earth!
Your glory is higher than the heavens.
You have taught children and infants to tell of your strength,
silencing your enemies and all who oppose you.
When I look at the night sky and see the work of your fingers –
the moon and the stars you set in place –
what are mere mortals that you should think about them,
human beings that you should care for them?
Yet you made them only a little lower than God
and crowned them with glory and honour.
You gave them charge of everything you made,
putting all things under their authority –
the flocks and the herds and all the wild animals,
the birds in the sky, the fish in the sea,
and everything that swims the ocean currents.
O Lord, our Lord,
your majestic name fills the earth!

Psalm 8, New Living Translation

Sunset over Kintyre

'Milky' Burn, Catacol, Isle of Arran

TO GOD
be the glory

*T*o God be the glory, great things He hath done,

So loved He the world that He gave us His Son,

Who yielded His life our redemption to win,

And opened the life-gate that all may go in.

Fanny Crosby (1820–1915)
An American Methodist mission worker and a prolific hymn writer.
She went blind as a child but still managed to write over 8,000 hymns.

HOW GREAT
Thou Art!

O Lord my God, when I in awesome wonder,

Consider all the works thy hands have made,

I see the stars, I hear the mighty thunder,

Thy power throughout the universe displayed;

Then sings my soul, my Saviour God, to thee:

How great thou art! How great thou art!

The Reverend Carl Boberg (1859–1940)
A Swedish clergyman, he was 25 years old when he wrote the lyrics of this hymn
after trekking two miles through a thunderstorm after a church meeting.
Translated by **Stuart K Hine** (1899–1989).

Prayers
FROM THE HEART

SIR JACOB'S
Prayer

O Lord,

you know how busy I must be this day.

If I forget you,

do not forget me.

Sir Jacob Astley (1579–1652)
Sir Jacob is said to have spoken this prayer before the Battle of Edgehill in 1642.
He had only just been made commander of the Royalist Infantry, as the Earl of
Lindsey stepped down from the position on the morning of the battle.

Prayer of a
BRETON FISHERMAN

Lord, the sea is so wide

and my boat is so small.

Be with me.

Anon

In Time of TROUBLE

*H*ear my prayer, O Lord,
And let my cry come to You.
Do not hide Your face from me
in the day of my trouble;
Incline Your ear to me;
In the day that I call,
answer me speedily.

Psalm 102:1-2, New King James Version

*In prayer it is better to have
a heart without words than
words without a heart.*
John Bunyan (1628–1688) British author,
best known for *The Pilgrim's Progress*.

Rowing boat at Lochranza

51

Swan at sunset

Prayer should be the key of the day and the lock of the night.
George Herbert (1593–1633), British metaphysical poet

Prayers
FOR THE EVENING

AS EVENING COMES

May the Lord support us all the day long

till the shades lengthen

and the evening comes,

and the busy world is hushed,

and the fever of life is over

and our work is done.

Then, in his mercy,

may he give us a safe lodging and a holy rest

and peace at the last.

John Henry Newman (1801–1890)
In 1845, Newman left the Church of England to join the Roman Catholic Church, where he was eventually granted the rank of cardinal by Pope Leo XIII. He was instrumental in the founding of the Catholic University of Ireland, which became Dublin University.

Gentle Jesus,
MEEK AND MILD

Gentle Jesus, meek and mild,

Look upon a little child;

Pity my simplicity,

Suffer me to come to Thee.

Fain I would to Thee be brought,

Dearest God, forbid it not;

Give me, dearest God, a place

In the Kingdom of Thy grace.

Charles Wesley (1707–1788)
A well-known leader of the Methodist movement in England, Wesley is chiefly
remembered for the many hymns he wrote. Many children grew up saying this
verse as a prayer at bedtime, though 'meek and mild' is perhaps not the
most accurate description of Jesus!

Keeping an eye on things, Arran

e to come to Thee • Fain I would to *Thee* be brought • Dearest God, *forbid* it not •

Sunset over Queen's Park Baptist Church, Glasgow

NIGHT VIGIL

*W*atch, dear Lord,

with those who wake,

or watch, or weep tonight,

and let your angels protect

those who sleep.

Tend the sick.

Refresh the weary.

Sustain the dying.

Calm the suffering.

Pity the distressed.

We ask this

for the sake of your love.

Saint Augustine of Hippo (354–430)
A philosopher and theologian from the
Africa Province of the Roman Empire. He is
generally considered as one of the greatest
Christian thinkers of all times. His writings
were influential in the development of
Western Christianity.

ABIDE WITH ME

*A*bide with me;

fast falls the eventide;

The darkness deepens;

Lord with me abide.

When other helpers fail

and comforts flee,

Help of the helpless,

O abide with me.

Henry Francis Lyte (1793–1847)
Lyte was inspired to write this hymn as
he was dying of tuberculosis; he finished
it in time for his farewell sermon to his
parish. He died just three weeks after
writing these words. 'Abide with me'
was King George V's favourite hymn.

ST AUGUSTINE'S
Prayer

I entrust the past to your mercy,
the present to your love,
and the future to your providence.

Saint Augustine of Hippo (354–430)

LIGHTEN OUR
Darkness

*L*ighten our darkness, we beseech Thee, O Lord;
and by thy great Mercy
defend us from all perils and dangers of this night;
for the love of Thy only Son,
our Saviour, Jesus Christ.

From *The Book of Common Prayer.*

Sunset over the Isle of Arran

Pray, and let God worry!

Martin Luther (1483–1546),
German monk, priest, professor of theology
and key figure in the Protestant Reformation.

Sunset on the water

TAPS

*D*ay is done, gone the sun,

From the lake,

from the hills,

from the sky;

All is well, safely rest, God is nigh.

Taps is a musical piece sounded at dusk, and at funerals. It is likely that the title, *Taps*, comes from the three drum taps that were played as a signal for 'Lights out' when a bugle was not used.

CLOSING
Prayer

*M*ay the grace of our Lord Jesus Christ,

and the love of God,

and the fellowship of the Holy Spirit

be with us all,

evermore.

Amen

Based on **2 Corinthians 13:13–14**